It is Human

To be

Cyclist

By

Marcks Rosales

Book	**It is Human to be Cyclist**
Author	**Marcks Rosales**
Copyright	
Book ISBN	**9798851425202**
Publication	**07 July 2023**

Preface

This book is aimed at all cyclists who in one way or another contribute to the decontamination of the planet, making their mobility an act of faith and affection for their family, their community and their species.

Index

Chapter I

Start the Day

Starting my daily routine as usual, it is possible that fatigue was present again, although this time I had to be more energetic and allow myself to reach my final destination earlier, I do not want to say at the end of my life, just arrive, how easy to say, being in the concrete jungle, where we did not find tigers, nor lions, but if cars and trucks, you do not know, sorry if I did not show up, I am Arameus and this time I will tell you all my adventures, I live in Lima-Peru, or in Mombaza-Kenya, or in Kathmandu-Nepal, which is the case in Latin America, heat, rain, dangerous curves and potholes are part of everyday life as they say that IT IS PART OF, yesterday I spent part of my day reading a battered newspaper that said they were looking for an expert in CAD drawing, I hope to get to take the square, of course if I am lucky, you know I have 8 children to support, it is not what I heard in a film by Arnold Schwarzenegger.

Continuing with my cycling prologue, it is difficult to drive or pedal for hours and in this abysmal, or rather animal, heat, at another point of my thinking, I would expect the Shiba **Inu crypto** to reach

the penny on the dollar, advice not requested, but if you want to start or dream someday of investing or rather be an investor in the stock market (Wall Street type), first practice or said so use cryptocurrencies, they are cheaper and your investment will be small, of course I clarify that the investment you make is with money that you allow yourself to lose and this is not investment advice, the streets or life on the planet becomes increasingly dangerous and I think that apart from the investment issue, you should also dedicate your time to practice some kind of discipline in self-defense, **Krav Maga or / and Jiu jitsu**, for my part, I am already starting it, although the practice must be a constant to climb in the perfection of these arts, I see a lot of female presence in these workshops, maybe it is due to the wave of constant mistreatment of women, crime will always attack the most defenseless or weak, crime does not pay and I hope that soon this ends, I do not want to live at levels of other countries, poverty in other countries should not be Maybe the **cause of more violence,   these gentlemen should dedicate themselves to work and not to harm the nation that shelters them or perhaps, is part of a plan and only seek to destroy the next country, to continue with the next,** it is sad to see what Latin America is becoming and it is curious that it always comes from countries where the **blood** doctrine is waved, it seems that the intention of this doctrine or political ideology is to impoverish each country, perhaps because they understand that if in Latin America, where natural resources swarm, border, excessive, this region will be much more powerful than the other existing ones.

Cyclist Diary

Chapter II

Manifesto to the Planet

I do not want to delve into reasons or deductions, but it seems to be of great interest that this part of the region is always in a state of war, of misery, because in this way the large groups can continue to support, in quotation marks, the poor nations of the world such as Africa or Latin America, which are the richest nations on the planet. **IT IS NOT EASIER TO TRY** that the whole earth prospers and we reach a level of global equality, I know that this must be the reality in another universe, but and in this part of our time and our universe, it is not possible, it is no longer just man taming the animal, now it is man taming man and that is reality.

I do not seek to decline your point of view, each one has its truth or, rather, **you will see things according to the crystal you use to SEE.**

But what do we do with the truth of a Country, or the truth of a **Nation** and the truth of a **Continent**, who will have the exclusivity of the truth, politicians, priests, big business, the media, power groups.

Or such that as happened in Mexico, the one of yesteryear is clear not the one of now.

As in the **one that Bernardo Borgoend** and mainly, the will of thousands of free Mexicans who left their home and family to defend their faith to the cry of **¡Viva Cristo Rey!** It was in the states of Jalisco, Guanajuato, Michoacán, San Luis Potosí, Zacatecas and Colima where the struggle had the greatest impact.

These Latinos fought for their belief, for their faith, and they didn't care about the power of government.

And they left a very big mark on Patria.

That is what compels me to the next question.

THAT THE STRONGEST, WITHIN THE HEART OF MAN, TRUTH OR FAITH.

A lonely man, a heart can only change a country, if this people stops making noise and listening to the beating of this man.

It is also true that information and the internet currently have a great or enormous influence on the population.

That control always existed, nobody denies that, the power that the church had was enormous and with that it was never better for humanity, it simply managed it according to the **PaPa** he ate, it is not if clergy.

It is also applicable advice that you are less and less dependent on the blessed system, **(THE BIG BROTHER OR RATHER THE MATRIX).**Even in this part of the planet, they still do not control us as much **as in the United States of America** (as the grenn-out likes), as a result of the events last September, the famous PATRIOT ACT was established in this nation, in which the state can enter your house, whenever it wants, Because intervention is indicated as a matter of national security.

And that's not bad, it's more blessed that you are USA, there is no crime in your country that you cannot repel, each nation is free to protect its citizens as it can and using the tools it requires.

I am more inclined to the belief that the world is governed by as a physical phenomenon, where it exists.

There is Action and Reaction,

There are poor and there are rich,

There are good guys and there are bad guys.

The idea is that balance serves us for good or to be more human and not just to bring out the animal side of our nature.

We must always remind ourselves that we are still human and not just one type of battery that works, is used and then discarded.

Or you think I'm less human.

Because I'm **Black**,

Because I was born in **Peru**,

Because I have **Indigenous** blood,

Because I'm from a developing country .

I am human only because I am your kind.

I think I'm human because I try to be better every day, because I think about creating a better world, because I make my world better, because I tell a stranger he's a champion, because I give water to a puppy, because I don't eliminate a bird, because I think of other beings as one.

Because I must not pollute my house, nor my mind, nor my neighborhood, nor my Fabela, nor the avenue, nor must I insult a curvy woman who wiggles like a road,

No, nou not, never,

I do, think and imagine all this and more when I get on a bike.

Cyclist Diary

Chapter III

At the End of the Route

Maybe it's too late, our lives are too short, if we compare ourselves to the life of the dinosaurs, which existed on our planet, let's not be that stone destroyed these reptiles and now destroys ourselves.

And let's start looking at both equally who is next to us.

Simplicity is the repetitive thing you find in these lines, but Prometheus get more exquisite in future editions.

I am a cyclist,

I am indigenous,

I'm black,

I am a Christian,

I am mestizo,

I am pro-animal,

I am redskin,

I am Indian,

I am human............ and even flesh and blood.

VOICE YOU WILL READ THE STORY, WITH ANOTHER PERSPECTIVE.

Chapter IV:

The Awakening of a Cyclist

Again Arameas opened his eyes slowly. Sunlight filtered through the window, illuminating his room. He got out of bed and walked over to the mirror. He looked at his reflection and was disappointed. His body was out of shape and he didn't look like a real cyclist. His muscles were limp and his belly was sticking out. He decided that today would be the day he would change his life and become a real cyclist.

On the first lap he dressed in his sportswear and headed for his bike. I had bought it a couple of years ago, but I had hardly used it. He climbed on it and started pedaling through his neighborhood. At first he struggled to keep up, but little by little he was improving. He arrived at a nearby park and stopped to rest. There he realized that he had come a good distance. He felt proud and decided to move on.

But then he received a painful call, Carmela his cat had died, trying to follow him, after a puppy scared her, she felt faint, she was a very small being to which she was very close, she was with 4.5 years, they shared many moments, you do not know how well a human gets along with another species, of course, they are years of domestication you say, that since Egyptian times, what do you say bambino, that I must put bandages and find out, not For a while kid, what better and will be happier my Carmelite, if I cremate her and leave her ashes to the sea.

That kitten was an adventurer, if I told you, the times we played, but finally now she is with her whole species in the kingdom of Bastet, I say it with great respect, of course, I only hope that in the world, which is now now, she is happier, than here on earth, on my part I did everything possible because her stay is prosperous and happy, If I know, it is a little difficult to understand a being that only meows you, although with different sound levels of course, I always thought that when she spoke to her she understood me, I think so, because after I sat in the room next to her, she always calmed down, she just wanted company and that he was next to her.

It is so easy to share like this with another being, it is phenomenon, kid.

Chapter V:

Training for Life

Arameus decided he needed a plan to become a real cyclist. He searched the internet for information and found a training program for beginners. He decided to follow him and vowed to do it every day. At first it was difficult, but little by little he felt stronger and more agile. His legs began to define and his abdomen became flatter. He felt excited and motivated to continue.

Then he and a group of cyclists began to notice that there were more people in his neighborhood who were also cyclists. He decided to approach them and join their group. He was a little intimidated at first, but soon realized that everyone was friendly and welcoming. He began to hang out with them on their tours and learn from their advice and experiences. He was grateful to have found a community that shared his passion.

He had a déjà vu and recalled that, as a child, the same thing happened in school and that he practices it constantly, he came to occupy one of the first positions in the subject that before, he failed, maybe that is part of the spark that every person needs to overcome and move to the other level, THE DIFFICULTY, If everything is ok in his comfort zone, he will never know that he needs sweat, sacrifice and effort to achieve satisfaction or improve.

It would be much more human if the struggle is not for a selfish achievement, but an achievement for your species, that should be the purpose of the new generations, if we live in our capsule, we will never know what others need, only what I, and I and then I need.

It is not an end of anything, that end will only lead to destruction.

And that you believe that is well known by those at the top and you will only do what they tell you.

Don't fall into its trap and try to get out of it today not tomorrow.

You're already 50 boy.....if it's not today when.

Chapter VI:

The challenge

One of the cyclists in the group proposed a challenge: a 50-kilometer race on a nearby mountainous route. He felt excited, but also a little nervous. He knew he wasn't fully prepared, but he decided to accept the challenge. He focused on his training and dedicated himself to improving his endurance and speed. The race was approaching and he was ready to do his best.

On the morning of the race, he met his group of cyclists and together they headed to the starting point. The route was steep and full of challenges, but our friend was determined to finish it. They cycled together for most of the way, supporting each other and encouraging each other.

Finally, they reached the finish line. Aramaeus was exhausted, but also full of joy. He had completed the 50-kilometer course in an impressive amount of time. He hugged his fellow riders and was grateful for their support and motivation. The race had been a success and he felt more motivated than ever to keep improving as a cyclist.

Chapter VII:
The lesson

At the end of the day, it was understood that reaching the goal is not only winning, but as life itself is a lesson learned.

He completed his cycling trip successfully. He covered hundreds of kilometers and faced many challenges, but he never gave up. He learned that being a cyclist wasn't just about pedaling, but also about perseverance and determination. He was grateful for the cycling community he had found and for the support he had received from his family and friends. He decided to continue pedaling and exploring the world from his bike. Being human, being a cyclist, became his life motto.

Part of our life is to travel our hours, days, years with people, days, events that modify, motivate, inspire others and ourselves, we never leave our route, our path is the one we must follow at all costs is part of our work in this life.

And if we do not do it well do not worry, you have an exact copy of yourself in another and other universes that will fulfill your mission or the challenges or desires that you always sought so that you do nothing, your other yooos will do it for you.

It is a cycling joke to follow on the road and there is little left, this acasito nomas.

Cyclist Diary